WILL STANDARDS SAVE
PUBLIC EDUCATION?

"New Democracy Forum operates at a level of literacy and responsibility which is all too rare in our time." —John Kenneth Galbraith

Other books in the NEW DEMOCRACY FORUM series:

WILL STANDARDS SAVE PUBLIC EDUCATION?

DEBORAH MEIER
FOREWORD BY JONATHAN KOZOL

EDITED BY JOSHUA COHEN AND JOEL ROGERS
FOR *BOSTON REVIEW*

BEACON PRESS
BOSTON

BEACON PRESS
25 Beacon Street
Boston, Massachusetts 02108-2892
www.beacon.org

Beacon Press books
are published under the auspices of
the Unitarian Universalist Association of Congregations.

05 04 03 02 01 00   8 7 6 5 4 3 2 1

This book is printed on recycled acid-free paper that contains at least 20
percent postconsumer waste and meets the uncoated paper ANSI/NISO
specifications for permanence as revised in 1992.

Composition by Wilsted & Taylor Publishing Services

Library of Congress Cataloging-in-Publication Data
Meier, Deborah.
     Will standards save public education? / Deborah Meier / edited by
Joshua Cohen and Joel Rogers for *Boston Review*.
          p.   cm. — (New democracy forum series)
     ISBN 0-8070-0441-3 (pbk.)
     1. Education—Standards—United States.   2. Educational tests
and measurements—United States.   I. Meier, Deborah.   II. Cohen,
Joshua.   III. Rogers, Joel.   IV. New democracy forum.

     LB3060.83.188 2000
     371.26'2—dc21

                                                     99-089137

CONTENTS

FOREWORD

JONATHAN KOZOL

Education writing, as John Holt observed when he and I were teaching high school English in the summer at the Urban School in Boston more than thirty years ago, is frequently a way of speaking indirectly of our own biographies and longings and unveiling our own souls. In speaking of "the aims of education" for a city or a nation, even for a neighborhood, we draw to some degree on who we are, and what we like (or don't like) in ourselves, and what we wish we might have been.

So when I listen to debates on education—whether about standards, pedagogic styles, or objectives, or "assessments," or whatever else—I listen first to voices. Before I pay attention to ideas, I want to gain some sense of character and value—lived experience—within the person who is telling us what he or she believes is best for children. I was an English literature student long before I was a teacher. I studied with Richard Poirier, John Hawkes, Walter Jackson Bate, and—for two years I will always treasure—in a seminar with Archibald MacLeish. They all knew something about voices. They knew how voices can reveal agendas.

I should say therefore, right at the start, that I have always liked the voice I hear when Deborah Meier speaks of children. She seldom speaks bombastically. She recognizes that we know less than we frequently pretend about the ways that children learn. She speaks without contempt for ambiguities and doesn't try to package certitudes simplistically.

Her style of thought reminds me sometimes of that of George Dennison, a writer and an educator and a friend from long ago, now in his grave, who worked in New York City for a time and worried constantly about the tensions between culture in a very grand, old-fashioned sense and human independence, freedom, and uniqueness. He was a literary man in all respects; we stayed up one night in a small hotel room that we shared, regaling one another with our favorite passages and characters in Tolstoy and Turgenev. But he was also very much concerned about the danger of approaching children with a bag of grown-up certitudes, with a compendium of "truths" and "absolutes"—approaching them, that is, not merely with a sensible adult authority but with a ruthlessness, an irresistible assertiveness, that sweeps all hesitation in the dust, as if to say, "I know what's good, because it's good for *me*, and I will damn well make you good in my own image."

Erik Erikson wrote in *Young Man Luther* of "the general problem of man's exploitability in childhood," including in this notion not just "overt cruelty" but other forms of injury such as "sly righteousness." He spoke of what he termed "the life principle of trust," without which, he said, "every human act, may it feel ever so good and seem ever so right, is prone to perversion by destructive forms of conscientiousness."

Destructive conscientiousness is what I hear in many of the voices of the less reflective advocates for uniformity in standards. I would add to this that I am not, by any means, *opposed* to "standards"—cultural or pedagogic—if, by standards, we are speaking of the willingness to state that certain areas of knowledge, certain disciplines of thinking, even certain facts and dates and concepts, even certain literary works, are more important, more worth learning, than some others. To act as if this were not so would be to abdicate our own adulthood.

I do think, to take an obvious example, that there's such a thing as "bad" and "good" and "better" when it comes to books for children or to any other facet of our cultural endowment. When I was teaching fourth grade in the Boston schools in 1965 and 1966, I refused to have my students read the poems of Whittier and Edgar Guest, which were on the lists of "standards" foisted on us by the school board then. I snuck in early poems of William Butler Yeats and some by John Crowe Ransom, and a few by Langston Hughes—in the latter case, not only because Hughes is African-American but also because he's a better poet than the ones the school system prescribed.

I still have biases, and I do not disguise them when I work with children. I can't abide a popular book series called *The Baby-sitters Club,* which third- and fourth-grade girls find irresistibly appealing; I slip them *Harriet the Spy* and *Charlotte's Web,* because I know they'll like these books once they get into them. I don't look over my shoulder and see Dennison or Holt chastising me. I know they did things like this too. Neither, ultimately, believed in utter anarchy.

So the question, for me, isn't if we ought to have some "standards" in our children's education. It is, rather, how and where they are determined, and by whom, and how they're introduced, and how we treat or penalize (or threaten, or abuse) the child or the teacher who won't swallow them. Many of the veteran teachers that I talk with in the schools of the South Bronx—and some of the young ones, too, who come into the classroom straight from college—have good taste, strong preferences, "high standards," if that is the term we need to use; but their standards aren't the same as those of E. D. Hirsch or William Bennett, or my own. They're often what I would call "maverick standards," not in cookie-cutter shapes, not on official lists, and never keyed to those obsessively enumerated particles of amputated skill associated with upcoming state exams.

Many of the teachers that I know in the South Bronx could teach in universities but *choose* to teach in elementary schools because they love the personalities of children and they also have a moral vision of a good society and want to do their part in bringing incremental bits of justice to an unjust city and an unjust world. They come with all the treasures they have gleaned from their own education. They want to share these treasures with the children, but they also want to find the treasures that exist already *in* those children, and they know they cannot do this if they're forced to march the kids in lockstep to the next "objective" or, God help us, the next "benchmark," so that they'll be ready—and God help us, please, a little more—to pass the next examination.

They worry about scripted journeys where there is no room for whimsical discoveries and unexpected learnings. They worry about outcomes that are stated in advance. They worry too about "efficiency" and "economic productivity" as the exclusive goals, or the commanding goals, of public education. Some of them recall another social order not so long ago that regimented all its children with remarkable success to march with pedagogic uniformity, efficiency, and every competence one can conceive—except for independent will—right into Poland, Austria, and France, and World War II. They worry about fascist intellection: streamlined, agile, uniform, competitive, but heartless and incapable of shrewd denunciation. They do not want to see a child, of whatever race or economic class, grow up to be as competently acquiescent as, for instance, Albert Speer—a man who, we may be quite sure, did very well on all his state exams.

These are teachers who have standards; but their standards may resemble those of Thomas Merton, or Thoreau, or Toni Morrison, more than of a market analyst or business CEO. The best teachers of little kids I know are poets in their personalities: they love the unpredictable. That's why they're drawn to children and not business school. If we force them to be little more than the obedient floor managers for industry, they won't remain in public schools. The price will be too high. The poetry will have been turned to prose: the worst kind too, the prose of experts who know every single thing there is to know except their own destructiveness.

In this way, we'll lose the teachers who come to the world of childhood with ministries of love and, in their place, we'll get technicians of proficiency. Test scores might improve a trifle for a time; if all you do is drill a kid, you do get something for your money, temporarily. Not a lot, though, and not over the long haul.

The better teachers understand these risks. That's why I listen closely to their voices. Then I listen to the voices of the experts and the politicians. By and large, I like the voices of the teachers better. Happily, however, there are still some experts who remember what it's *like* to be a teacher. Ted Sizer still remembers; and, for this, a generation of young teachers have been grateful. So too does William Ayers. That, I suspect, is why I find their voices in this little book enlivening, humane, and generous.

I am less attracted to the voice of Abigail Thernstrom. It has a hard edge, sharp with cleverness and adversarial malevolence. It's a shame, because I find, to my surprise, I actually agree with part of what she says. Without a grounding in substantial knowledge, she observes, you can't embark on intellectual adventures: not, in any case, the really interesting ones. I'd add to this that, without any grounding in substantial knowledge, a critical consciousness is of embarrassingly little use: You end up being not a smart dissenter but a clumsy one; and no one listens to your views because they're intermixed with ignorance and error.

So the question, again, is not if we "need" standards in our schools but with what sensibilities we navigate between the two extremes of regimented learning with destructive overtones, on one side, and pedagogic aimlessness and fatuous romanticism on the other. Somewhere between the world of Dickens's Gradgrind and John Silber and the world of pedagogic anarchy, there is a place of sanity where education is intense and substantive, and realistically competitive in a competitive society, but still respectful of the infinite variety of valued learnings and the limitless varieties of wisdom in the hearts of those who come to us as students.

It's in that place that Deborah Meier has been working all these years. Her voice conveys a life of struggle in the front lines—victories and losses, hopes and disappointments—and a seasoned recognition of how hard it is to make a difference in the years God gives us. It's a voice that's seldom harsh, and never overbearing, but humane and principled and wise; and it's a voice our nation needs to hear.

EDITORS' PREFACE

JOSHUA COHEN AND JOEL ROGERS

The current crop of freshmen in Massachusetts high schools will not graduate unless they pass the new Massachusetts Comprehensive Assessment System tests. This stringent requirement puts Massachusetts (along with New York) at the extreme end of a national movement to impose uniform educational standards on schools and "high-stakes" tests to assess whether students meet these standards. The details of this educational standardization remain open, but however they are filled in, the result is likely to have fateful consequences for public schools, and for the next generation of Americans.

In the lead essay in this New Democracy Forum, Deborah Meier, who has been a teacher and principal at innovative schools in New York City and Boston, argues that standardization threatens disaster for democracy. Schools, Meier maintains, teach democratic virtues: personal responsibility, tolerance, and how people who disagree with one another can still make sensible collective decisions. Moreover, schools provide this instruction by example: students learn the qualities of democratic citizenship by observing responsible adults who exhibit those qualities. Standardization threatens this instruction, Meier believes, by shifting authority over education to outside bodies, and turning teachers and principals into the vehicles for decisions taken elsewhere.⟩

Ted Sizer, Linda Nathan, and William Ayers share Meier's concerns, with Nathan describing how her own school (Boston Arts Academy) has established demanding local standards without external imposition. In contrast, Bob Chase, Gary Nash, Frank Murnane, and Abigail Thernstrom think Meier is too dismissive of common standards, and too trusting of local schools. Such standards, they argue, are needed for educational equity: they make schools accountable, and such accountability is especially important in poorer communities, where schools are now failing their students. But Meier's critics divide in their judgments about the practical consequences of current reform efforts. Thernstrom already detects benign effects; Nash, Chase, and Murnane remain more skeptical.

Equal opportunity is arguably the central value of American democracy, and schooling is essential to achieving it. So divisions over the right way to provide quality education are likely to provoke intense political fights. This Forum marks out the terrain of those coming battles.

1

EDUCATING A DEMOCRACY

DEBORAH MEIER

In the past two years, the number of students expelled from elementary and secondary schools in Chicago has nearly doubled. Expelled kids get sent to something called "safe schools," run by for-profit organizations. When a reporter asked Chicago officials why the number of spaces in the for-profit academies was far smaller than the number of expelled students, the reporter was reassured. Not to worry. They don't all show up. Meanwhile, the city is writing new categories and new zero-tolerance policies to push reform along. Chicago is the home of get-tough reform, and all these changes have been made in the name of upgrading "standards." The results? Test scores over the past three years have risen, we are told, by 3.4 percent in Chicago. That's a few more right answers on a standardized test, maybe.

Back in my home state of Massachusetts, the town of Lynnfield announced that it was time to end METCO, a program that for twenty years brought minority children into nearly all-white, middle-class, suburban communities. The board members explained to the press that the program wasn't helping the Lynnfield schools raise their "standards"—that is, their scores on the new tough state tests. Sometimes equity and excellence just don't mix well. So sorry.*

The stories of Chicago and Lynnfield capture a dark side of the "standards-based reform" movement in American education: the politically popular movement to devise national or state-mandated standards for what all kids should know, and high-stakes tests and sanctions to make sure they all know it. The stories show how the appeal to standards can mask and make way for other agendas: punishing kids, privatizing public education, giving up on equity.

I know how advocates of the movement to standardize standards will respond: "Good reform ideas can always be misused. Our proposals are designed to help kids, save public education, and ensure equity."

I disagree. Even in the hands of sincere allies of children, equity, and public education, the current push for far greater standardization than we've ever previously attempted is fundamentally misguided. It will not help to develop young minds, contribute to a robust democratic life, or aid the most vulnerable of our fellow citizens. By shifting the locus of authority to outside bodies, it undermines the capacity of schools to instruct by example in the qualities of mind that

---

* Eventually, Lynnfield backed off and decided to keep METCO but impose more stringent standards on METCO students than on others—a decision that prompted METCO to cut off its relationship with Lynnfield.

schools in a democracy should be fostering in kids—responsibility for one's own ideas, tolerance for the ideas of others, and a capacity to negotiate differences. Standardization instead turns teachers and parents into the local instruments of externally imposed expert judgment. It thus decreases the chances that young people will grow up in the midst of adults who are making hard decisions and exercising mature judgment in the face of disagreements. And it squeezes out those schools and educators that seek to show alternate possibilities, explore other paths.

The standardization movement is not based on a simple mistake. It rests on deep assumptions about the goals of education and the proper exercise of authority in the making of decisions—assumptions we ought to reject in favor of a different vision of a healthy democratic society. Drawing on my experience in schools in New York City and Boston, I will show that this alternative vision isn't utopian, even if it might be messy—as democracy is always messy.

Standards-Based Reform

Standards-based reform systems vary enormously in their details. But they are generally organized around a set of four interconnected mechanisms: first, an official document (sometimes called a framework) designed by experts in various fields that describes what kids should know and be able to do at given grade levels in different subjects; second, classroom curricula—commercial textbooks and scripted programs—that are expected to convey that agreed-upon knowledge; third, a set of assessment tools (tests) to measure whether children have achieved the goals specified in the framework; and fourth, a scheme of rewards and penalties directed at schools and school systems, but ultimately at individual kids, who fail to meet the standards as measured by the tests. Cutoff points are set at various politically feasible points—in some states they are pegged so that nearly 90 percent of the students fail, whereas other states fail less than 10 percent. School administrators (and possibly teachers) are fired if schools fail to reach particular goals after a given period of time, and kids are held back in a grade, sent to summer school, and finally refused diplomas if they don't meet the cutoff scores.

Massachusetts, for instance, has recently devised tests in English, mathematics, history, and science (to be followed by other subjects over time) covering the state's mandated frameworks. The tests are given in grades four, eight, and ten. Beginning in 2003, students will need to pass the grade-ten tests to get a Massachusetts high school diploma; moreover, the tests are intended to serve as the sole criterion for rating schools, for admission to public colleges, and for as many other rewards and sanctions as busy state officials can devise.

The Massachusetts tests are not typical; each state has its own variant. The Massachusetts tests are unusually long (fifteen to twenty hours), and cover a startling amount of territory. For fourth graders the history and social studies portions allow the test makers to ask questions about any-thing that happened between prehistoric times and A.D. 500 in "the world" and in the United States until 1865. While world history expands in the upper grades, a student can get a high school diploma without ever studying U.S. history af-ter 1865. The science and math portions are equally an inch deep and a mile wide. And the selections and questions on the reading tests were initially designed with full knowledge (and intent) that if scores did not immediately improve 80 percent of all fourth graders would fail, even though Massa-chusetts fourth graders rank near the top in most national reading assessments.

But the specifics of the tests are not the central issue. Even if they were replaced by saner instruments, they would still embody a fundamentally misguided approach to school reform. To see just how they are misguided, we need first to ask about their rationale. Why are these tests being im-posed?

Why Standards?

Six basic assumptions underlie the current state and na-tional standard-setting and testing programs now off the ground in forty-nine of fifty states (all but Iowa):

1. Goals: It is possible and desirable to agree on a single definition of what constitutes a well-educated eighteen-year-old and demand that every school be held to the same definition. We have, it is argued, gotten by without such an agreement at a great cost—witness the decline of public education—in comparison with other nations with tight national systems.

2. *Authority:* The task of defining "well-educated" is best left to experts—educators, political officials, leaders from industry and the major academic disciplines—operating within a system of political checks and balances. That each state's definition at the present time varies so widely suggests the eventual need for a single national standard.

3. *Assessment:* With a single definition in place, it will be possible to measure and compare individuals and schools across communities—local, state, national, international. To this end, curricular norms for specific ages and grades should be translated into objective tests that provide a system of uniform scores for all public, and if possible private, schools and districts. Such scores should permit public comparisons between and among students, schools, districts, and states at any point in time.

4. *Enforcement:* Sanctions, too, need to be standardized, that is, removed from local self-interested parties, including parents, teachers, and local boards. Only a more centralized and distant system can resist the pressures from people closest to the child—the very people who have become accustomed to low standards.

5. *Equity:* Expert-designed standards, imposed through tests, are the best way to achieve educational equity. While a uniform national system would work best if all students had relatively equal resources, equity requires introducing such

a system as rapidly as possible regardless of disparities. It is especially important for schools with scarcer resources to focus their work, concentrating on the essentials. Standardization and remotely controlled sanctions thus offer the best chance precisely for underfunded communities and schools, and for less well educated and less-powerful families.

6. *Effective Learning:* Clear-cut expectations, accompanied by automatic rewards and punishments, will produce greater effort, and effort—whether induced by the desire for rewards, fear of punishment, or shame—is the key to learning. When teachers as well as students know what constitutes failure, and also know the consequences of failure, a rational system of rewards and punishments becomes an effective tool. Automatic penalties work for schooling much as they do for crime; consistency and certainty are the keys. For that reason compassion requires us to stand firm, even in the face of pain and failure in the early years.

A Crisis?

The current standards-based reform movement took off in 1983 in response to the widely held view that America was at extreme economic risk, largely because of bad schools. The battle cry, called out first in *A Nation at Risk,* launched an attack on dumb teachers, uncaring mothers, social promotion, and general academic permissiveness. Teachers and a new group labeled "educationists" were declared the main enemy, which undermined their credibility, and set the stage for cutting them and their concerns out of the cure. According to critics, American education needed to be reimagined, made more rigorous, and, above all, brought under the control of experts who, unlike educators and parents, understood the new demands of our economy and culture. The cure might curtail the work of some star teachers and star schools, and it might lead, as the education chief of Massachusetts recently noted, to a lot of crying fourth graders. But the gravity of the long-range risks to the nation demanded strong medicine.

Two claims were thus made: that our once-great public system was no longer performing well, and that its weaknesses were undermining America's economy.

Most critics have long agreed that the data in support of the claim about school decline are at best weak (see Richard Rothstein's 1998 book, *The Way We Were?*). As a result, the debate shifted, although the average media story hardly noticed, to an acknowledgment that even if there wasn't a decline in school achievement, the demands of the new international economy required reinventing our schools anyway. Whether the crisis was real or imagined, change was required. But efforts to induce changes in teaching and learning met with widespread resistance from many different quarters: from citizens, parents, teachers, and local officials. Some schools changed dramatically, and some changed bits and pieces, but the timetable was far too slow for the reformers. The constituents who originally coalesced around *A*

Nation at Risk began to argue that the fault lay either in the nature of public schooling itself or in the excesses of local empowerment. The cure would have to combine more competition from the private or semiprivate sector and more rigorous control by external experts who understood the demands of our economy and had the clout to impose change. This latter viewpoint has dominated the standards-based reform movement.

Unfortunately, a sense of reality has been lost in these shifting terms of debate. Now, fifteen years (more or less) after analysts discovered the great crisis of American education, the American economy is soaring, the productivity of our workforce is probably tops in the world, and our system of advanced education is the envy of the world. In elementary school literacy (where critics claim that sentimental pedagogues have for decades failed to teach children how to read), the United States still ranks second or third, topped only by one or another of the Scandinavian countries. While we rank lower in math and science tests, we continue to lead the world in technology and inventiveness. If the earlier argument was right and economic prowess requires good schooling, then teachers in America ought to be congratulated, and someone should be embarrassed by the false alarm. Instead, the idea that schools are a disaster, and that fixing them fast is vital to our economy, has become something of a truism. It remains the excuse for all reform efforts, and for carrying them out on the scale and pace proposed.

Educators from the progressive tradition are often accused of "experimenting" on kids. But never in the history of the nation have progressives proposed an experiment so drastic, vast, and potentially serious in its real-life impact on millions of young people. If the consequences are other than those its supporters hope for, the harm to the nation's educational system and the youngsters involved—maybe even to our economy—will be large and hard to undo.

The Real Crisis

The coalition of experts who produced *A Nation at Risk* were wrong when they announced the failure of American public education and its critical role in our economic decline. Constructive debate about reform should begin by acknowledging this misjudgment. It should then also acknowledge the even bigger crisis that schools have played a major part in deepening, if not actually creating, and could play a big part in curing. This crisis requires quite a different set of responses, often in direct conflict with standardization.

An understanding of this other crisis begins by noting that we have the lowest voter turnout by far of any modern industrial country; we are exceptional for the absence of responsible care for our most vulnerable citizens (we spend less on child welfare—baby care, medical care, family leave—than almost every foreign counterpart); we don't come close to other advanced industrial countries in income equity; and our high rate of (and investment in) incarceration places us in a class by ourselves. All of these, of course, affect some citizens far more than others: and the heaviest burdens fall on the poor, the young, and people of color.

These social and political indicators are suggestive of a crisis in human relationships. Virtually all discussions, right or left, about what's wrong in our otherwise successful society acknowledge the absence of any sense of responsibility for one's community and of decency in personal relationships. An important cause of this subtler crisis, I submit, is that the closer our youth come to adulthood the less they belong to communities that include responsible adults, and the more stuck they are in peer-only subcultures. We've created two parallel cultures, and it's no wonder the ones on the grown-up side are feeling angry at the way the ones on the other side live and act: seemingly footloose and fancy-free but in truth often lost, confused, and knit together for temporary self-protection. The consequences are critical for all our youngsters, but obviously more severe—often disastrous—for those less identified with the larger culture of success.

Many changes in our society aided and abetted the shifts that have produced this alienation. But one important change has been in the nature of schooling. Our schools have grown too distant, too big, too standardized, too uniform, too divorced from their communities, too alienating of young from old and old from young. Few youngsters and few teachers have an opportunity to know each other by more than name (if that); and schools are organized such that "knowing each other" is nearly impossible. In these settings it's hard to teach young people how to be responsible to others, or to concern themselves with their community. At best they develop loyalties to the members of their immediate circle of friends (and perhaps their own nuclear family). Even when teens take jobs their fellow workers and their customers are likely to be peers. Apprenticeship as a way to learn to be an adult is disappearing. The public and its schools, the "real" world and the schoolhouse, young people and adults, have become disconnected, and until they are reconnected no list of particular bits of knowledge will be of much use.

In my youth there were over 200,000 school boards. Today there are fewer than 20,000, and the average school, which in my youth had only a few hundred students, now holds thousands. At this writing, Miami and Los Angeles are in the process of building the two largest high schools ever. The largest districts and the largest and most anonymous schools are again those that serve our least-advantaged children.

Because of the disconnection between the public and its schools, the power to protect or support them now lies increasingly in the hands of public or private bodies that have no immediate stake in the daily life of the students. CEOs, federal and state legislators, university experts, presidential think tanks, make more and more of the daily decisions about schools. For example, the details of the school day and year are determined by state legislators—often down to minutes per day for each subject taught, and whether Johnny gets promoted from third to fourth grade. The school's budget depends on it. Site-based school councils are increasingly the "in" thing, just as the scope of their responsibility narrows.

Public schools, after a romance with local power, beginning in the late 1960s and ending in the early 1990s, are increasingly organized as interchangeable units of a larger state organism, each expected to conform to the intelligence of some central agency or expert authority. The locus of authority in young people's lives has shifted away from the adults kids know well and who know the kids well—at a cost. Home schooling or private schooling seems more and more the natural next step for those with the means and the desire to remain in authority.

Our school troubles are not primarily the result of too easy course work or too much tolerance for violence. The big trouble lies instead in the company our children keep—or, more precisely, don't keep. They no longer keep company with us, the grown-ups they are about to become. And the grown-ups they do encounter seem less and less worthy of their respect. What kid, after all, wants to be seen emulating people he's been told are too dumb to exercise power, and are simply implementing the commands of the real experts?

Alternative Assumptions

Just as the conventional policy assumptions emerge naturally from a falsely diagnosed crisis, so does the crisis I have sketched suggest an alternative set of assumptions.

1. Goals: In a democracy, there are multiple, legitimate definitions of "a good education" and "well-educated," and it is desirable to acknowledge that plurality. Openly differing viewpoints constitute a healthy tension in a democratic, pluralistic society. Even where a mainstream view (consensus) exists, alternate views that challenge the consensus are critical to the society's health. Young people need to be exposed to competing views, and to adults debating choices about what's most important. As John Stuart Mill said, "It is not the mind of heretics that are deteriorated most, by the ban placed on all inquiry which does not end in the orthodox conclusions. The greatest harm is done to those who are not heretics, and whose whole mental development is cramped, and their reason cowed, by the fear of heresy."

2. Authority: In fundamental questions of education, experts should be subservient to citizens. Experts and laymen alike have an essential role in shaping both ends and means, the what and the how. While it is wise to involve experts from both business and the academy, they provide only one set of opinions, and are themselves rarely of a single mind. Moreover, it is educationally important for young people to be in the company of adults—teachers, family members, and other adults in their own communities—powerful enough to decide important things. They need to witness the exercise of judgment, the weighing of means and ends by people they can imagine becoming; and they need to see how responsible adults handle disagreement. If we think the adults in children's lives are, in Jefferson's words, "not enlightened enough to exercise their control with a wholesome discretion, the remedy is not to take it from them, but to inform their discretion by education."

3. Assessment: Standardized tests are too simple and simpleminded for high-stakes assessment of children and schools. Important decisions regarding kids and teachers should always be based on multiple sources of evidence that seem appropriate and credible to those most concerned. These are old testing truisms, backed even by the testing industry, which has never claimed the level of omniscience many standards advocates assume of it. The state should require only that forms of assessment be public, constitutionally sound, and subject to a variety of "second opinions" by experts representing other interested parties. Where states feel obliged to set norms—for example, in granting state diplomas or access to state universities—these should be flexible, allowing schools maximum autonomy to demonstrate the ways they have reached such norms through other forms of assessment.

4. Enforcement: Sanctions should remain in the hands of the local community, to be determined by people who know the particulars of each child and each situation. The power of both business and the academy are already substantial; their access to the means of persuasion (television, the press, and so forth) and their power to determine access to jobs and higher education already impinge on the freedom of local communities. Families and their communities should not be required to make decisions about their own students and their own work based on such external measures. It is sufficient that they are obliged to take them into account in their deliberations about their children's future options.

5. Equity: A fairer distribution of resources is the principal means for achieving educational equity. The primary national responsibility is to narrow the resource gap between the most and least advantaged, both between 9 A.M. and 3 P.M. and during the other five sixths of their waking lives when rich and poor students are also learning—but very different things. To this end publicly accessible comparisons of educational achievement should always include information regarding the relative resources that the families of students, schools, and communities bring to the schooling enterprise.

6. Effective Learning: Improved learning is best achieved by improving teaching and learning relationships, by enlisting the energies of both teachers and learners. The kinds of learning required of citizens cannot be accomplished by standardized and centrally imposed systems of learning, even if we desired it for other reasons. Human learning, to be efficient, effective, and long-lasting, requires the engagement of learners on their own behalf, and rests on the relationships that develop between schools and their communities, between teachers and their students, and between the individual learner and what is to be learned.

No "scientific" argument can conclusively determine whether this set of assumptions or the set sketched earlier is true. Although some research suggests that human learning is less efficient when motivated by rewards and punishments, and that fear is a poor motivator, I doubt that further research will settle the issue. But because of the crisis of human relationships, I urge that we consider the contrary claims rather more seriously than we have. We may even find that in the absence of strong human relationships rigorous intellectual training in the most fundamental academic subjects cannot flourish. In a world shaped by powerful centralized media, restoring a greater balance of power between local communities and central authorities, between institutions subject to democratic control and those beyond their control, may be vastly more important than educational reformers bent on increased centralization acknowledge.

An Alternative Model

Suppose, then, we think about school reform in light of these alternative assumptions. What practical model of schools and learning do they support? In brief, our hope lies in schools that are more personal, compelling, and attractive than the Internet or TV, where youngsters can keep company with interesting and powerful adults who are in turn in alliance with the students' families and local institutions. We need to surround kids with adults who know and care for our children, who have opinions and are accustomed to expressing them publicly, and who know how to reach reasonable collective decisions in the face of disagreement. That means increasing local decision making, and simultaneously decreasing the size and bureaucratic complexity of schools. Correspondingly, the worst thing we can do is to turn teachers and schools into the vehicles for implementing externally imposed standards.

Is such an alternative practical? Are the assumptions behind it mere sentiment?

At the Mission Hill in Boston, one of ten new Boston public schools initiated by the Boston Public Schools and the Boston Teachers Union, we designed a school to support such alternative practices. The families who come to Mission Hill are chosen by lottery and represent a cross section of Boston's population. We intentionally keep the school small with fewer than two hundred students ages five to thirteen—so that the adults can meet regularly, take responsibility for each other's work, and confer and argue over how best to get things right. Parents join the staff not only for formal governance meetings, but for monthly informal suppers, conversations, good times. Our oldest kids, the eighth graders, will graduate only when they can show us all that they meet our graduation standards, which are the result of lots of parent, staff, and community dialogue over several years.

All our students study—once when they are little, once when they are older—a schoolwide interdisciplinary curriculum. Last fall they all became experts on Boston and Mission Hill, learning its history (and their own), geography, architecture, distinct neighborhoods, and figures of importance. Last winter they all re-created ancient Egypt at 67 Allegheny Street. This coming winter they will re-create ancient China. Each spring they dig into a science-focused curriculum theme. The common curriculum allowed us, for example, to afford professional and amateur Egyptologists, who joined us from time to time as lively witnesses to a life-long passion. We have a big central corridor that serves as our public mall, where kids paint murals and mix together to read and talk across ages. High school youngsters who share the building with us read with little ones, take them on trips, and generally model what it can mean to be a more responsible and well-educated person.

We invented our own standards, not out of whole cloth but with an eye to what the world out there expects and what we deem valuable and important. And we assess them through the work the kids do and the commentary of others about that work. Our standards are intended to deepen and broaden young people's habits of mind, their craftsmanship, and their work habits. Other schools may select quite a different way of describing and exhibiting their standards. But they too need to consciously construct their standards in ways that give schooling purpose and coherence, and then commit themselves to achieving them. And the kids need to understand the standards and their rationale. They must see school as not just a place to get a certificate, but a place that lives by the same standards it sets for them. Thus the Mission Hill school not only sets standards but has considerable freedom and flexibility with regard to how it spends its public funds and organizes its time to attain them. All ten pilot schools offer examples of different ways this might play out, ways that could be replicated in all Boston schools.

Standard setting and assessment are not once-and-for-all issues. We reexamine our school constantly to see that it remains a place that engages all of us in tough but interesting learning tasks, nourishes and encourages the development of reasonable and judicious trust, and nurtures a passion for making sense of things and the skills needed to do so. We expect disagreements—sometimes painful ones. We know that even well-intentioned, reasonable people cross swords over deeply held beliefs. And we know, too, that these differences can be sources of valuable education when the school itself can negotiate the needed compromises.

What is impressive at Mission Hill, at the other pilot schools, at the Central Park East School in New York's east Harlem, where I worked for twenty-five years, and the thousands of other small schools like them, is that over time the kids buy in. These schools receive the same per capita public funding as other schools receive, are subject to city and state testing, and must obey the same basic health, safety, and civil rights regulations. But because these schools are small, the families and faculties are together by choice, and all concerned can exercise substantial power over staffing, scheduling, curriculum, and assessment, the schools' cultural norms and expectations are very different than those of most other public schools.

The evidence suggests that most youngsters have a sufficiently deep hunger for the relationships these schools offer them—among kids and between adults and kids—that they choose school over the alternative cultures on the Net, tube, and street. Over 90 percent of Central Park East's very typical students stuck it out, graduated, and went on to college. And most persevered through higher education. Did they ever rebel, get mad at us, reassert their contrary values and adolescent preferences? Of course. Did we fail with some? Yes. But it turns out that the hunger for grown-up connections is strong enough to make a difference if we give it a chance. Studies launched in New York between 1975 and 1995 conducted on the other similar schools show the same pattern of success.

Standards, yes. Absolutely. But as Theodore Sizer, who put the idea of standards on the school map in the early 1980s, also told us then: we need standards held by real people who matter in the lives of our young. School, family, and community must forge their own, in dialogue with and in response to the larger world of which they are a part. There will always be tensions; but if the decisive, authoritative voice always comes from anonymous outsiders, then kids cannot learn what it takes to develop their own voice.

I know this "can be" because I've been there. The flowering of so many new public schools of choice over the past two decades proves that under widely different circumstances, very different kinds of leadership and different auspices, a powerful alternative to externally imposed standards is available.

And I also know the powerful reasons why it "can't be"— because I've witnessed firsthand the resistance even to allowing others to follow suit, much less encouraging or mandating them to do so. The resistance comes not simply from bad bureaucrats or fearful unions (the usual bogeymen), but from legislators and mayors and voters, from citizens who think that if an institution is public it has to be all things to all constituents (characterless and mediocre by definition), and from various elites who see teachers and private citizens as too dumb to engage in making important decisions. That's a heady list of resisters.

But small self-governing schools of choice, operating with considerable flexibility and freedom, also resonate with large numbers of people, including many of those who are gathering around charter schools, and even some supporters of privatization and home schooling. They too come from a wide political spectrum and could be mobilized.

Accountability

And yet doubts about accountability will linger. In a world of smaller, more autonomous schools not responsible to centralized standardization, how will we know who is doing a good job and who isn't? How can we prevent schools from claiming they're doing just fine, and having those claims believed, when they may not be true? Are we simply forced to trust them, with no independent evidence?

What lies behind these worries? For those who buy into the conventional assumptions, anything but top-down standardization seems pointless. But for those whose concern is more practical there are some straightforward and practical answers to the issue of accountability that do not require standardization.

To begin with, I am not advocating the elimination of all systems for taking account of how schools and students are doing. In any case, that is hardly a danger.

Americans invented the modern, standardized, norm-referenced test. Our students have been taking more tests more often than any nation on the face of the earth, and schools and districts have been going public with test scores starting almost from the moment children enter school. For the third- or fourth-grade level (long before any of our international counterparts bother to test children) we have test data for virtually all schools, by race, class, and gender. We know exactly how many kids did better or worse in every subcategory. We have test data for almost every grade there-after in reading and math, and to some degree in all other subjects. This has been the case for nearly half a century. Large numbers of our eighteen-year-olds now take standardized college entry tests (SATs and ACTs). In addition, the national government now offers us its own tests—the NAEP—which are given to an uncontaminated sample of students from across the United States and now reported by grade and state. And all of the above is very public.

In addition, public schools have been required to produce statements attesting to their financial integrity—how they spend their money—at least as rigorously as any business enterprise. They are held accountable for regularly re-porting who works for them and what their salaries are. In most systems there are tightly prescribed rules and regula-tions; schools are obliged to fill out innumerable forms re-garding almost every aspect of their work: how many kids are receiving special education, how many incidents of vio-lence, how many suspensions, how many graduates, what grades students have received, how many hours and minutes they study each and every subject, and the credentials of their faculties. This information, and much more, is public. And the hiring and firing of superintendents has become a very common phenomenon.

In a nation in which textbooks are the primary vehicle for distributing knowledge in schools, a few major textbook publishers, because of a few major state textbook laws, dom-inate the field, offering most teachers and schools (and students) very standardized accounts of what is to be learned, and when and how to deliver this knowledge. Moreover, most textbooks have always come armed with their own end-of-chapter tests, increasingly designed to look like the real thing; indeed, test makers also are the publishers of many of the major standardized tests.

In short, we have been awash in accountability and standardization for a very long time, but we are missing precisely the qualities that the last big wave of reform was intended to respond to: teachers, kids, and families who know each other or each other's work and take responsibility for it; we are missing communities built around their own articulated and public standards and ready to show them off to others.

The schools I have worked in and support have shown how much more powerful accountability becomes when one takes this latter path. The work produced by Central Park East students, for example, is collected regularly in portfolios, and it is examined (and in the case of high school students, judged) by tough internal and external reviewers, in a process that closely resembles a doctoral oral exam. The standards by which a student is evaluated are easily accessible to families, clear to kids, and capable of being judged by other parties. In addition schools such as this undergo schoolwide external assessments that take into account the quality of their curriculum, instruction, staff development, and culture as well as the impact of the school on students' future success (in college, work, and so forth).

Are the approaches designed by Central Park East or Mission Hill the best way? That's probably the wrong question. We never intended to suggest that everyone should follow our system. It would be nice if it were easier for others to adopt our approach; it would be even better if it were easier—in fact required—for others to adopt alternatives to it, including the use of standardized tests if they so choose. My argument is for more local control, not for one true way.

I opt for more local control not because I think the larger society has no common interests at stake in how we educate all children, or because local people are smarter or intrinsically more honorable. The interests of wider publics are important in my way of thinking. I know that pressure exists at Mission Hill to not accept or push out students who are difficult to educate, who will make us look worse on any test, or whose families are a nuisance. It's a good thing that others are watching us to prevent such exclusion.

But the United States is now hardly in danger of too much localized power. (The only local powers we seem to be interested in expanding are those that allow us to resegregate our schools by race or gender.) What is missing is balance—some power in the hands of those whose agenda is first and foremost the feelings of particular kids, their particular families, their perceived local values and needs. Without this balance my knowledge that holding David over in third grade will not produce the desired effects is useless knowledge. So is my knowledge of different ways to reach him through literature or history. This absence of local power is bad for David's education and bad for democracy. A backseat driver may be more expert than the actual driver, but there are limits to what can be accomplished from the rear seat.

In short, the argument is not about the need for standards or accountability, but what kind serves us best. I believe standardization will make it harder to hold people accountable and harder to develop sound and useful standards. The intellectual demands of the twenty-first century, as well as the demands of democratic life, are best met by preserving plural definitions of a good education, local decision making, and respect for ordinary human judgments.

EDUCATION AND DEMOCRACY

If we are to make use of what we knew in Dewey's day (and know even better today) about how the human species best learns, we will have to start by throwing away the dystopia of the ant colony, the smoothly functioning (and quietly humming) factory where everything goes according to plan, and replace it with a messy, often rambunctious, community, with its multiple demands and complicated trade-offs. The new schools that might better serve democracy and the economy will have to be capable of constantly remaking themselves and still provide for sufficient stability, routine, ritual, and shared ethos. Impossible? Of course. So these schools will veer too far one way or the other at different times in their history, will learn from each other, shift focus, and find a new balance. There will always be a party of order and a party of messiness.

If schools are not all required to follow all the same fads, maybe they will learn something from their separate experiments. And that will help to nurture the two indispensable traits of a democratic society: a high degree of tolerance for others, indeed genuine empathy for them, as well as a high degree of tolerance for uncertainty, ambiguity, and puzzlement, indeed enjoyment of them.

A vibrant and nurturing community, with clear and regular guideposts—its own set of understandings, its people with a commitment to one another that feels something rather like love and affection—can sustain such rapid change without losing its humanity. Such a community must relish its disagreements, its oddballs, its misfits. Not quite families, but closer to our definition of family than of factory, such schools will make high demands on their members and have a sustaining and relentless sense of purpose and coherence, but will be ready also to always (at least sometimes) even reconsider their own core beliefs. Their members will come home exhausted, but not burned out.

Everything that moves us toward these qualities will be good for the ideal of democracy. A democracy in which less than half its members see themselves as "making enough difference" to bother to vote in any election is surely endangered—far more endangered, at risk, than our economy. It's for the loss of belief in the capacity to influence the world, not our economic ups and downs, that we educators should

{ 30 }

accept some responsibility. What I have learned from thirty years in small powerful schools is that it is here above all that schools can make a difference, can alter the odds.

We can't beat the statistical advantage on the next round of tests that being advantaged has over being disadvantaged; we can, however, substantially affect the gap between rich and poor where it will count, in the long haul of life. Even there it's hard to see how schools by themselves can eliminate the gap, but we can stop enlarging it. The factory-like schools we invented a century ago to handle the masses were bound to enlarge the gap. But trained mindlessness at least fit the world of work so many young people were destined for. We seem now to be reinventing a twenty-first-century version of the factory-like school—for the mindworkers of tomorrow.

It is a matter of choice; such a future does not roll in on the wheels of inevitability. We have the resources, the knowledge, and plenty of living examples of the many different kinds of schools that might serve our needs better. All we need is a little more patient confidence in the good sense of "the people"—in short, a little more commitment to democracy.

2

NO EXCUSES

ABIGAIL THERNSTROM

What an alarming picture: expelled students in Chicago, unwanted black youngsters in Lynn, vulnerable urban kids terribly harmed by the demand that they meet state academic standards. What on earth can Massachusetts and so many other states be thinking of?

Of course, those Chicago students may be troublemakers keeping everyone else from learning; they may need the "safe schools" that have been specially designed for them. In Massachusetts, meanwhile, the METCO program has never been properly evaluated for its academic impact on the minority students—who are, after all, far from a random sample of the Boston school population. Sure, they go to college in high numbers, but, most likely, that would have been equally true had they stayed in Boston. If we want to talk about equity, let's discuss all of Boston's students, not just those who have been privileged to ride a bus to the suburbs. They all deserve a good education, which is precisely what the current drive for high academic standards and accountability is about.

Indeed, the reforms that Deborah Meier scorns have been inspired, first and foremost, by concern for highly disadvantaged kids, who for so long have been educationally neglected. And already in Massachusetts the new demands are driving better instruction. For instance, for years Boston promoted students who had not mastered the most basic reading and math skills; the district is now talking about strategies to teach reading to those who arrive in high school functionally illiterate. It's running a catch-up summer school. Many districts are placing new emphasis on early intervention to rescue children already behind by second grade; some are running summer workshops in content areas for teachers; others are adding more reading and writing to their curricula, since the tests ask open-ended questions that assess the student's ability to understand complex material and organize a short essay.

The demand for academic rigor is changing teaching in the tony suburbs too. But it's not the kids in Lexington and Concord who will gain the most from the new stress on solid skills and a basic knowledge of core subjects. Deborah Meier wants different standards for advantaged and disadvantaged children. Instead, the state is delivering a vital message: no excuses. Kids can come from low-income, one-parent families, or from chaotic neighborhoods. The color of their skin may be a few shades darker than that of an Irish Catholic. But in the classroom, it doesn't matter. They can still be expected to acquire the knowledge and skills they will need to hold down decent jobs in today's economy. And knowledge and skills are the road to true equality.

Low expectations are demeaning and patronizing, and let's not kid ourselves about the basic economic picture.

Meier is concerned about "income equity." Increasingly since the early 1980s, those who know more, earn more. Not the number of years spent in school, but actual skills determine earnings. Word knowledge, paragraph comprehension, arithmetical reasoning, mathematical understanding: these are some of the skills the state-wide assessments measure, and they are the same skills that middle-class jobs require.

Deborah Meier suggests the definition of "well-educated" is up for grabs, that there is no consensus on what an eighteen-year-old should know. Does she really want to argue about the worth of learning geometry or the importance of understanding why we fought a civil war? And how about a nine-year-old? Would she label the insistence that kids read abhorrent "standardization"? Should the state remain unconcerned when a child does badly on a third-grade assessment? No one is talking about punishment; the point is to provide help. And to do so before the child begins to slip further and further behind, becomes discouraged, and tunes out.

The kids in her school were learning to read, she would undoubtedly argue. Not to worry. Trust her. Well, aside from the fact that her students at the Mission Hill school performed below the state average on the third-grade reading test, what is the principle here? In setting academic standards, should we trust everyone involved in every school, including the children themselves? Unencumbered by the road map that the state provides, will they magically all decide to drive in a good educational direction?

In fact, what's all this romantic stuff about schools freed from "outside" educational arbiters in order to do their own thing teaching kids basic democratic values—responsibility for one's own ideas, tolerance for others, the capacity to negotiate differences? Totally severed from the state, some schools may engage in racist admissions practices, teach intolerance, and celebrate armed conflict. And that's just for starters. Public dollars carry strings. That's what Title VI of the 1964 Civil Rights Act is all about: accept federal money, and you can't discriminate. Accountability is now tied to state education funds as well. Schools that the taxpayers fund must meet the standards that those taxpayers and their representatives set. If Deborah Meier doesn't like strings, she ought to advocate the complete privatization of education—an idea from which she surely recoils. Or she should campaign to send educationally deprived students to one of the parochial schools that are serving inner-city children so well, free from heavy-handed government interference. She's a closet no-strings voucher advocate.

Meier sees standards as a threat to individuality. But the highly educated are the most radical individuals of all in American society—just cast an eye over the Harvard faculty. The educational system in France could hardly be more centralized, and the French don't look like lemmings to me. Knowledge is liberating, not confining. And you can't embark on an intellectual adventure, say, exploring the still-unanswered questions about World War II, unless you have a solid grounding in European history, the immediate German context, and the chronology of the conflict. Yes, learning requires digesting, even memorizing, some basic knowledge. But that knowledge, once acquired, becomes the springboard from which the imaginative individual takes off.

Meier's essay contains much rhetoric about "democracy" and "community." She even throws in "commitment" and "love." Nice buzzwords. They warm our hearts. But how do our new academic standards stop the creation of smaller, more nurturing schools that are tied to the local neighborhood? And how do they threaten the fabric of American democratic life? (She draws a lurid link between statewide standards and low turnout on election day. Quite a stretch.) Thriving democracies require educated citizens. And educating citizens is what ed reform is all about.

MAKING A DIFFERENCE

BOB CHASE

Deborah Meier has definitely hit a raw nerve. It is teachers, after all, who must implement the new state-mandated standards. These standards are typically imposed by politicians and education policy experts in state capitals, far away from the realities of our classrooms. To teachers, the standards movement increasingly looks like an exercise in political grandstanding, perpetrated by people who haven't been in a real classroom for years, rather than a serious effort to improve the quality of education.

Is it any wonder that teachers are enormously frustrated? I agree with much of what Deborah Meier advocates, and always have. We absolutely must decrease the size and bureaucratic complexity of schools. We must empower teachers. We must truly connect with children, especially those on the brink of adulthood. Those youngsters need more than peer-only subcultures and the instant gratification of the market; they need responsible adults, with solid values, involved in their lives. But I do not accept Deborah Meier's premise that any standards created outside of an individual school by a state or school district will necessarily make matters worse.

I believe standards can work—they can lead to improved student learning—if a number of conditions can be met. First of all, the standards must reflect the wisdom of parents and classroom teachers. Second, the curricula we teach must be aligned with the new standards. Third, teachers must be provided the professional development they need to incorporate the new standards into their teaching practice. Fourth, we all must insist that no single high-stakes test can measure the academic progress of any student—that multiple indicators must be employed.

Finally, and most important, we must pursue higher academic standards with our eyes wide open. The objective of the standards movement—to successfully educate all children, rich and poor, to the same high standards—is truly revolutionary. We must match our revolutionary intentions with commensurably revolutionary interventions to ensure that all students, especially underprivileged students, succeed. It is intellectually and morally dishonest to raise the bar for all students to a level that is currently being reached by only a relative few, unless governments at all levels are willing to undertake an unprecedented effort to reduce class sizes, put a qualified teacher in every classroom, and upgrade school facilities.

Unfortunately, the prevailing mind-set among too many politicians and policy makers is something right of out *Field of Dreams:* "If we set high standards, students will magically achieve." They are deluding themselves. The fact is that poor and minority students are far more likely to attend schools with noncertified teachers, large class sizes, and substandard learning resources due to the *savage inequalities* (to use Jonathan Kozol's apt term for the disparities between inner-city and suburban schools) of today's schools. Yet the politicians who want to "get tough" on schools seem to expect disadvantaged students to achieve, by fiat, the same high ambitious standards achieved by privileged students. If the standards movement does not provide ample *means* for all students to meet higher academic expectations, it will prove to be one of the cruelest hoaxes in American history, right up there with Horatio Alger.

In her book, *Other People's Children*, educator Lisa Delpit argues that "the upper and middle classes send their children to schools with all the accouterments of the culture of power; children from other kinds of families operate within perfectly wonderful and viable cultures, but not cultures that carry the codes or rules of power." And she takes today's educators to task for watering down curricula and academic expectations when teaching children who come from outside this "culture of power." What's more, Delpit reports that educators often fail to teach these children—the urban and rural working-class and poor—the skills, including spoken and written language codes, that they need to succeed in the larger society. I see the standards movement as perhaps a once-in-a-lifetime opportunity to rectify this situation across many school districts.

Public school is, or should be, the place where hope becomes capacity. A student with a high school diploma should be able to go directly into the world of work, and participate fully in his or her job and community. And the high school graduate who goes on to college, as a majority now do, should be capable of doing college-level work without any remedial education. These two goals should be the foundation of any effort to formulate new standards.

Our schools should be making it possible for students to exceed the income and educational limitations of their class and family. That has always been one of the highest and noblest ambitions of public education in our democracy. And that's certainly what public education did for me. Now the great challenge is for the schools to make a real difference in every child's life.

EXPERT OPINION

GARY B. NASH

I write this response to Deborah Meier's indictment of the standards-based "reform movement" as someone who was deeply involved in constructing the National History Standards for United States and world history and at the same time a critic of the California History Standards. While I agree mostly with Meier's concern about what has happened in Massachusetts in the last few years, and almost entirely with her principles regarding education in a democracy, I believe she is much too categorical in her criticism of what is happening nationally in standards-based reforms. Particularly distressing is her disdain for the efforts of university-based scholars to involve themselves in K-12 education.

Among the hundreds of teachers, administrators, and academic historians involved in constructing the National History Standards, there was a general agreement, clearly stated in the introduction to the published standards, that they were meant "to promote equity in the learning opportunities and resources to be provided all students in the nation's schools." The standards were meant to provide guidelines, and perhaps some inspiration, for those interested in (1) "defining for all students the goals essential to success in a rapidly changing global economy and in a society undergoing wrenching social, technological, and economic change" and (2) "establishing the moral obligation to provide equity in the educational resources required to help all students attain these goals." Those who constructed the National History Standards (teachers, academic historians, and curriculum specialists) knew that they would have little effect in raising historical literacy across the country unless teachers were better trained in subject areas, unless rich curricular material was available in all the schools, and unless equity was established in the public schools where inequities are glaring.

Meier believes that standards-based education has led to standardization that has shifted "the locus of authority to outside bodies" and turned "teachers and parents into the local instruments of externally imposed expert judgment." What has happened in Massachusetts gives her plenty of reasons for such a view. As Dan French, a leader of the state's department of education has spelled out, a vigorous, forward-looking, and highly participatory attempt to create discipline-based standards was undermined by a sudden change in political leadership.* When Governor William Weld put John Silber in the driver's seat, he scuttled the work of thousands of teachers and parents and replaced their efforts with a rigid, prescriptive framework that has placed "innovative schools and teachers" (of the sort that

---

* "The State's Role in Shaping a Progressive Vision of Public Education," *Phi Delta Kappan* (November 1998).

Deborah Meier leads) "in the difficult position of having to modify their full curricula in order to align them with the new standards."

The Massachusetts standards are indeed lamentable. It is absurd to hold students at the fourth-grade level responsible for world history to A.D. 500 and U.S. history until 1865. And if Meier is correct that Massachusetts state tests based on these standards will be the single criterion for rating schools and admitting students to Massachusetts public colleges, then I join her in protest. Meier is wrong, however, to believe that authority exercised at the state level in creating standards cannot work to the advantage of equity in the schools. French's view, one that I share, is that in a society stratified along racial and economic lines "the absence of [state] standards guarantees that educational opportunities for students will be stratified according to where one lives and what one's background is."

Meier offers a scary vision of centralized authority where "experts"—she defines them as "educators, political officials, leaders from industry and the major academic disciplines"—have been busily suppressing teacher innovation and democratic education. This is a caricature of how discipline-based national standards were constructed and how they work at the state and local levels. History, math, science, and other discipline-based standards vary widely from state to state (Iowa has opted to have none) in the skill with which they have been constructed and in the degree to which they are mandated to operate at the district or school level. In California, for example, sturdy history standards have been constructed through a long and sometimes contentious process, and local schools have constructed their own standards which have drawn on the National History Standards as well as the California state standards. In Fairfax County, Virginia, teachers and curriculum specialists have constructed a fine set of history standards, precisely because they found the state standards unacceptable. Around the nation, cities and school districts do not blindly follow "externally imposed" standards. Rather, they are writing their own. Meier's description of public schools as "increasingly organized as interchangeable units of a larger state organism, each expected to conform to the intelligence of some central agency or expert authority," bears little resemblance to how public education works in California, or in many other states where I have worked in an effort to improve history instruction in K-12 schools.

What especially dismays me is Meier's linking of officious centralized agencies of educational authority with "academic expertise." For one thing, state departments of education are not necessarily backward looking; that wasn't the case in Massachusetts when the standards-making process began. But more to the point, why does Meier so distrust academic experts in subject areas? A major problem in history education in the last half century is that professional historians walked away from involvement in K-12 education. Now they are returning from "the long walk." For example, the National History Standards Project drew upon the expertise of dozens of specialists in the many fields and eras of world and U.S. history, and the academic historians worked closely, cooperatively, and cordially with the teacher task forces involved. It is hard to imagine how history standards faithful to the best scholarship of the last several generations would have been constructed without this expertise. Does Meier really want to mirror William Buckley's classic statement that he would trust the first one hundred names in the Boston telephone directory over the faculty at Harvard University on almost any topic? Where is the evidence that "university experts," whom she lumps together with corporate "CEOs, federal and state legislators, [and] presidential think tanks," are making "more and more of the daily decisions about schools"? Her argument that "in fundamental questions of education experts should be subservient to citizens" reminds me of Chester Finn's advice to the thirty national organizations that participated in building the National History Standards that "if Joe Six-pack in Dubuque, Iowa, doesn't like them, they aren't going anywhere." Finn's view was roundly dismissed by groups as varied as National Catholic Education Association, the Council of the Great City Schools, and the National Congress of Parents and Teachers.

Are national standards setting and national assessments around the corner, as Meier seems to believe? None of the national standards—in civics, geography, science, math, history, the arts, and economics—was ever imagined to be a mandatory national standard. The standards were constructed for those who cared to look at them for guidance in building state or local standards or refashioning individual school curricula. That is how they have been used. Every state and district I have encountered is grateful for them. As for national assessments, is there any evidence that either political party is plumping for this? In a nation dedicated for several centuries to locally controlled education, high-stakes national assessments are not going to appear any time soon.

(Meier believes in local control and local empowerment. So do I—to a degree.)But the United States also has a long history of vicious and retrograde local school boards. Meier's position awkwardly places her in company with many figures on the religious right who aim to control local school boards in order to banish evolution in science classrooms, scrap critical thinking, circumscribe world history, and reinstitute prayer in the schools. Local control cuts both ways—for progressive or retrograde education. In her own school, she seems to have found local empowerment strategies possible in spite of the misguided attempts of Weld and Silber to reconstitute public education. So perhaps the balance between central authorities and local communities is working better than she allows.

HABITS OF MIND

LINDA NATHAN

The Boston Arts Academy faculty has just finished a long discussion about the "habits of mind" of our graduates. It has taken us eighteen months to come to a consensus about these habits, as well as about the content and skill standards in our academic and arts disciplines. These conversations have been invigorating, intense, and often very difficult. But ultimately they have helped us pinpoint what we think it is important for our graduates to know and be able to do when they leave our school.

First, we grouped together by subject area (humanities, science, math, world languages, student support, arts) to discuss the essential skills (what students should be able to do) and the essential content (what students should know) a high school graduate ought to attain. After reaching agreement in each of these areas, we tried to define the habits or orientations we wanted all our students to possess. What kinds of questions did we want all our students to be able to ask? What kinds of behaviors or attitudes toward academic and artistic disciplines did we want for our students? And, perhaps most important, what kind of civic behavior or responsibility did we want all our students to demonstrate? After deciding on our skill standards, we worked backward and asked each other about the habits of mind that we wanted to instill in our students.

At different points in the process, we asked parents for their input. We initially asked parents to describe the skills and content that was important to them for their children to master. We initially wondered whether parents would have enough background or information to even engage in this discussion, so we were pleased that their goals for their children closely matched our teachers' goals for their students. And although many of our students are only fourteen, and don't have a particularly "long" view of education, they, too, have been helpful in setting standards for their own learning.

For now we have agreed on the following habits: invention, connection, refinement, and ownership. These are not proposed in a linear order, but rather as large concepts for us to imbed in our teaching. For each large concept or habit we ask a series of questions to help define that habit.

For "invention" we ask: What is my passion and how do I use it in my work? Do I take risks and push myself? What makes this work special? How do I nourish my creativity? How can I extend or play with what is given to me? What further questions could I pursue? What further possibilities could I see? How inventive am I when challenged by something difficult?

For "connection" we pose: Who is my audience and how do I connect my work to the audience? What am I trying to say? What can I draw from in my own personal experience?

What else does this work connect to? How could I interpret or analyze this work? Why does this work matter? When is work "good"? Is this approach the only one possible? What are the implications of this approach? What is the work's purpose or importance?

Considering the habit of "refinement," we ask: What tools do I need? Have I demonstrated good craftsmanship? What are my strengths and weaknesses? When is the work finished? What further skills do I need? Have I demonstrated understanding? Have I conveyed my message?

And for "ownership": How does this work affect others? What or whom is this work for? How do I find the drive to go on? What do I need to be successful? How do I approach a project and follow through? How do I advocate for my work and the work of others? What am I working for? How do I cope with frustration? How do I know when to ask for help and what is the most effective way to ask? Am I proud to stand behind my work? Am I committed to my work?

We are a relatively small faculty of thirty-five. Nevertheless, it was not easy to achieve consensus about these habits. In fact, it was not easy to achieve consensus about the very term *habits of mind*. To some of us, the word *habits* had negative connotations and sounded too rigid. Others wanted stronger links to John Dewey and the idea of progressive education. All of us wanted habits that would apply to both the academic and artistic realms since our students spend at least ten hours a week in an art discipline. Formulating the questions that surround and define each habit helped us to focus on the kind of graduates we want.

Now, it is our job is to make these habits and our standards come alive in all our classrooms. Otherwise, our work will merely be laundry lists of "things to master" that will not have real meaning to anyone. After all, the point of having agreed-upon standards is so that they can play a vigorous role in the school community. It is fairly meaningless to have a list of science standards if neither teachers nor students and parents have made any serious connection to "owning" those standards. For us, habits of mind have become the framework with which to approach the learning of standards. If you possess the habits of a good learner, then the learning of content makes so much more sense. Otherwise, you run the risk of just accumulating facts that you will forget after the next test. At the Boston Arts Academy we want graduates who possess the habit of invention, the habit of refining work, the habit of making connections, and, last, but certainly not least, the habit of ownership. The work must matter to the maker, and the maker must take responsibility for the making of the work.

How will this approach help our students on the MCAS? The MCAS, as Meier eloquently explains, are essentially an antidemocratic tool. Rather than provide a suggestive and lean set of descriptors for what Massachusetts youngsters should know and be able to do, the state has set up a system of mandated curricula that follows the laundry list approach of learning a myriad of isolated facts. In fact, the state has prevented schools from adopting an integrated science curriculum combining biology, chemistry, and physics with increasing complexity each year—an idea put forward by the National Academy of Sciences, and other preeminent science educators. For students to master the MCAS in tenth grade, there can be only one prescribed way to teach science. Is this really the approach we want for our children?

I think that we, as parents and educators, have allowed the politicians and policy makers to go too far. Rather than demanding that the state take responsibility for establishing minimum standards in literacy and mathematics, we have allowed the state to declare war on all schools and all teachers (and all students). I am not interested in schools that take the most important decisions about learning out of the hands of those closest to the learners: the teachers. When the state gets in the business of giving schools endless laundry lists that must be taught, we lose our ability to teach well.

I applaud Deborah Meier's six alternative assumptions for what make good schools. Her last assumption is one that I believe is a truth: "Improved learning is best achieved by improving teaching and learning relationships." This is ultimately how students, and teachers, learn best. We must be engaged in order to learn well and for that learning to have the kind of long-lasting effect that we hope will sustain our democratic society. Otherwise, why have schools at all?

None of this is to say that the state should not be in the business of assessing some aspects of student learning. I think it is worthwhile for the state to demonstrate inequities in learning and then to provide helpful strategies for improvement. It is important for us, in this commonwealth, to note that students in Wellesley do better on standardized tests than do students in Boston. However, the solution to this inequity is not to mandate twenty-five more hours of testing (as the state currently does). This will only increase the inequity. The solution is more costly, more labor-intensive, and has more to do with social change than education reform. If Boston is to compete with Wellesley, we must have smaller class sizes, a longer school day, and high-quality academic, arts, and physical education. We must have a well-educated teaching force with opportunities for professional development and a limit of eighty students per teacher (at least at the secondary level). If Boston is to compete with Wellesley, we must have the same quality school libraries as found in the suburbs so that all of our students can read the same wonderful books. We must have clean classrooms, bathrooms, and playgrounds. We must have enlightened leadership in our schools. We must have summer programs that enforce academic skills while providing enrichment opportunities. But a twenty-hour test? How does this help our students?

As for Meier's alternative model, I object only to the word *alternative*. I don't see her model, the model I have experienced and found such success with, as alternative. I see this model as the only way our schools will continue our traditions of democracy and public schools for all young people. I invite our education policy makers and legislators to visit schools like Boston Arts Academy, Central Park East, and Mission Hill. Then they will understand the kind of education that is possible for all young people.

THE CASE FOR STANDARDS

RICHARD J. MURNANE

Contrary to Debbie Meier's view, I believe that standards-based educational reforms have significant promise for improving the quality of American public education. Moreover, I believe they are critical to reducing educational inequalities that have left many American families with insufficient earnings to support their children.

I want to make clear that I have enormous respect for Debbie Meier as an educator. Central Park East, which she started, is a remarkable school. I also agree with many of Debbie Meier's criticisms of current versions of standards-based reforms. Yet I see America's children better served by making standards-based reforms work than by scrapping the concept.

The real earnings of thirty-year-old American male high school graduates are 20 percent lower today than the earnings of the comparable group twenty years ago. This is in part because changes in the economy have made skills more important determinants of earnings today than they were in the past. While the skills of today's high school graduates are not lower, on average, than those of high school graduates twenty years ago, they are not high enough to meet the needs of high-wage employers today. Since a high school diploma does not guarantee that a graduate has mastered any particular set of skills, employers offering good jobs typically bypass high school graduates in favor of college graduates. One consequence is that students not planning on college have little incentive to do the hard work required to master certain skills.

Black males have suffered particularly much as a result of changes in the economy. In 1990, thirty-year-old black males earned, on average, less than 80 percent of what white males of the same age earned. More than two thirds of this gap can be explained by the difference in the measured cognitive skills of the two groups. This is a legacy of the low-quality schools so many black American children attend, schools where the standards for what children are expected to learn are much lower than standards that typically prevail in suburban schools.

Weak skills leave many graduates of American schools, especially students from low-income families and minority groups, with an enormous handicap when competing for jobs in an economy that increasingly values skills. I view this as a significant threat to the stability of our democracy.

Standards-based educational reforms are quite new in America. They were preceded by twenty years of state legislatures trying to alter the financing of local public education without much interference with local control. In most states, the finance reforms led to a large increase in state government funding of public education, especially to communities with relatively small tax bases and relatively high property tax rates. If these communities had kept local funding for education constant, the net effect would have been significant equalization of per pupil spending. But this did not occur. Instead, local communities substituted state funding for local school funding, then cut property taxes. The net result was much greater equalization of property tax rates than of education funding.

At least part of the explanation for this pattern is demographic: the percentage of families in the United States with children under the age of eighteen has fallen in the last forty years. As a result, the constituency for high-quality education has become smaller relative to the constituency for tax relief. School finance reform did result in spending increases in some communities. But additional expenditures did not lead consistently to student achievement increases. In some cases, the money was used for patronage. In other cases, it was spent on fragmented programs that had little effect on how teachers taught and what students learned. In the absence of good information about their children's skills, parents were at a significant disadvantage when arguing with other local groups about how educational resources should be spent.

The disappointing results of traditional school finance reforms led states to design initiatives in standards-based educational reforms, the goal of which was to focus on students' achievement rather than on simply providing money to local communities for education. I would add one point to Meier's list of the components of standards-based reforms: this is a commitment to providing teachers with the skills required to help all students meet the standards. Historically, most professional development funds have paid for one-day workshops that do not affect how teachers teach and students learn. A key element of any reform should be focusing professional development on helping teachers to teach critical skills more effectively.

Evidence of several varieties supports the notion that standards-based reforms can result in improved teaching and greater student learning. In California and in New York City's District 2 professional development linked closely with well-defined learning goals for children has produced tangible changes in how teachers teach and increased student achievement. In Texas low scores on state-mandated achievement tests have enabled community organizers to mobilize parents in low-income communities to demand improvements in their children's schools. And more than one hundred schools serving low-income children have banded together into the Alliance Schools Network, which is focused on improving education. While faculties and parents in these schools attempt to learn from each other, their concern about scores on standardized tests has not led to standardization of schooling. Rather, they are coming to understand that each school must develop its own strategy for helping all children to master critical skills.

I do not mean to imply that all is well with standards-based reform efforts. In many states, including Massachusetts, the standards have become much too detailed and the tests too burdensome. The assessments in many states are not varied enough in format to provide opportunities for students to demonstrate different dimensions of critical skills. In some schools, too much time is spent on developing test-taking skills instead of other forms of learning.

Another problem lies in determining the appropriate stakes. In some states, students with low scores are compelled to attend summer school, and students whose scores remain low are denied high school diplomas. In others, the jobs of teachers and administrators in schools with low scores are jeopardized. In some states, students in schools with low scores are given vouchers to attend schools of their choice. In still others, the scores are simply explained to local residents, and then residents decide what the appropriate response should be. It is not at all clear how teachers, students, and parents will respond to different combination of incentives, and how the responses will affect student achievement. It is critical to learn how stakes will affect the achievement of students of color and students from low-income families—groups that historically have fared poorly in American schools.

Meier believes that the problems with current versions of

standards-based reforms are so severe that the concept should be scrapped. I reach a different conclusion because I see that the enormous inequality in American education has been largely a legacy of local control. Significant increases in state education funding implemented through grants that left local control unhampered have reduced this inequality only modestly. I also see a number of states, including Kentucky, North Carolina, and Texas, learning as they gain experience with standards-based reforms. For example, over a decade Kentucky has changed significantly student learning goals and the methods used to assess students' skills. It has also altered the consequences associated with low test scores and improved its professional development strategies. The net effect has been significant increases in student achievement.

Individual states, including Massachusetts, still have much to learn about how to make standards-based educational reforms work. It is by no means certain that standards-based reforms will lead to better education in all of them. Yet, from the dire consequences of educational inequalities, the failure of traditional school-financing reforms to reduce these inequalities, and the cautious progress of standards-based reforms in some states, I believe that persevering with standards-based reforms makes sense. I propose two complementary tests that standards-based reforms should pass. The first is that the accountability system make it impossible for schools to continue to provide low-quality instruction to children from low-income families and minority groups. The second is that the accountability system not prevent distinguished educators such as Deborah Meier from creating and sustaining schools that provide a remarkably good education.

THE STANDARDS FRAUD

WILLIAM AYERS

The goals of school reform—to provide every child with an experience that will nourish and challenge development, extend capacity, encourage growth, and offer the tools and dispositions necessary for full participation in the human community—are simple to state but excruciatingly difficult to enact. Hannah Arendt once argued, "Education is the point at which we decide whether we love the world enough to assume responsibility for it and by the same token save it from that ruin which, except for renewal, except for the coming of the new and the young, would be inevitable . . . and where we decide whether we love our children enough not to expel them from our world and leave them to their own devices, nor to strike from their hands their chance of undertaking something new, something unforeseen by us, but to prepare them in advance for the task of renewing a common world." That's a lot, much of it dynamic and ever-changing, much of it intricately interdependent. Yet it is what we must seek, if our ideal is education in a democracy.

Today, there is no more insistent or attractive distraction from that ideal than the "standards movement" that Deborah Meier takes on. This conservative push, dressed up as a concern for standards, is at its heart a fraud. It promotes a shrill and insistent message, simple and believable in its own right, while it subtly shifts responsibility away from the powerful, making scapegoats of the victims of power.

High academic standards (as well as social and community standards) are essential to good schools, and such standards, in part, demonstrate a commitment to high expectations for all students. A watered-down curriculum, vague or meaningless goals, expectations of failure—these are a few of the ingredients of academic ruin, and they have characterized urban schools for too long. Standards exist, whether or not we are explicit about them, and standards of some sort are everywhere. I'm all for clarity of standards, for a more explicit sense of what we expect from students. The questions, however, are: What do we value? What knowledge and experience are of most worth? How can we organize access to that worthwhile knowledge and experience? When we look at this school or classroom, what standards are being upheld? Who decides? These kinds of deep and dynamic questions are never entirely summed up, never finished; they are forever open to the demands of the new. Standards setting, then, should not be the property of an expert class, the bureaucrats, or special interests. Rather, standard setting should be part of the everyday vocation of schools and communities, the heart and soul of education, and it should engage the widest public. Standard setting means systematically examining and then reexamining what we care about, what we hope for, what the known demands of us next. Standard setting, often by other names, is already the work of successful schools and many, many effective classrooms.

The "standards movement" is flailing at shadows. All schools in Illinois, for example, follow the same guidelines: these standards apply to successful schools as well as collapsing ones. These written, stated standards have been in place for decades. And yet Illinois in effect has created two parallel systems—one privileged, adequate, successful, and largely white; the other disadvantaged in countless ways, disabled, starving, failing, and African-American. Some schools succeed brilliantly while others stumble and fall. Clearly something more is at work here.

The American school crisis is neither natural nor uniform, but particular and selective; it is a crisis of the poor, of the cities, of Latino and African-American communities. All the structures of privilege and oppression apparent in the larger society are mirrored in our schools. Chicago public school students, for example, are overwhelmingly children of color and children of the poor. More than half of the poorest children in Illinois (and over two thirds of the bilingual children) attend Chicago schools. And yet Chicago schools must struggle to educate children with considerably fewer human and material resources than neighboring districts have. For example, Chicago has fifty-two licensed physics teachers in the whole city, and a physics lab in only one high school. What standard does that represent?

In the last two years, 50,000 kids attended summer school in Chicago in the name of standards. Tens of thousands were held back a grade. It is impossible to argue that they should have been passed along routinely—that has been the cynical response for years. But failing that huge group without seriously addressing the ways school has failed them—that is, without changing the structures and cultures of those schools—is to punish those kids for the mistakes and errors of all of us. Further, the vaunted standard turns out to be nothing more than a single standardized test, a relatively simpleminded gate designed so that half of those who take it must not succeed.

The purpose of education in a democracy is to break down barriers, to overcome obstacles, to open doors, minds, and possibilities. Education is empowering and enabling; it points to strength, to critical capacity, to thoughtfulness and expanding capabilities; it leads to an ability to work, to contribute, to participate. It aims at something deeper and richer than simply imbibing and accepting existing codes and conventions, acceding to whatever is before us. The larger goal of education is to assist people in seeing the world through their own eyes, interpreting and analyzing through their own experiences and thinking, feeling themselves capable of representing, manifesting, or even, if they choose, transforming all that is before them. Education, then, is linked to freedom, to the ability to see and also to alter, to understand and also to reinvent, to know and also to change to world as we find it. Can we imagine this at the core of all schools, even poor city schools?

If city school systems are to be retooled, streamlined, and made workable, and city schools are to become palaces of learning for all children (and why shouldn't they be?), then we must fight for a comprehensive program of change. Educational resources must be distributed fairly. Justice—the notion that all children deserve a decent life, and that those in the greatest need deserve the greatest support—must be our guide. There is no single solution to the obstacles we face. But a good start is to ask what each of us wants for our own children. What are our standards? I want a teacher in the classroom who is thoughtful and caring, not a mindless clerk or deskilled bureaucrat but a person of substance, depth, and compassion. I want my child to be seen, understood, challenged, and nourished. I want to be able to participate in the community, to have some voice and choice in the questions the school faces.

And so the set of principles outlined by Meier are useful. A small school—as metaphor and practice—is a good starting point. Better yet, one where school people find common cause with students and parents, remaking schools by drawing on strengths and capacities of communities rather than their deficiencies and difficulties. Such a school must focus on shared problems, and find solutions that are collective and manageable. It must talk of solidarity rather than "services," people as self-activated problem solvers and citizens rather than passive "clients" or "consumers." And it must focus on the several deep causes of school failure: the inequitable distribution of educational resources, the capacity of a range of self-interested bureaucracies to work against the common good, and the profound disconnect between schools and the communities they are supposed to serve.

The solutions to the problems we face in a democracy are, as Meier appropriately puts it, more democracy. If the standards guiding schools today are weak or watery—and in many instances they are—the answer is not silence, credulousness, and passivity, but a broader and deeper and more lively engagement with the widest possible public. This is messy and complicated, but true to the ideal of letting the people decide. School is a public space where the American hope for democracy, participation, and transformation collides with the historical reality of privilege and oppression, the hierarchies of race and class. We should all work to raise expectations for our children, to reform and restructure schools, to prepare all students for a hopeful and powerful future, to drive resources to the neediest communities, to demand successful and wondrous learning environments for everyone, to involve teachers, parents, and communities—the public in public schools—in the discussion of what's important for kids to know and experience. At that point the conservative "standards movement," geared to simple, punitive, one-size-fits-all solutions, can be swept aside for something so much better.

A SENSE OF PLACE

THEODORE SIZER

A national "summit" meeting on the reform of elementary and secondary education was held several years ago at the conference center of a Fortune 500 corporation and involved fifty governors and fifty business leaders, each chosen from his state by its governor. The president of the United States and his secretary of education were the 101st and 102nd conferees.

The meeting was, apparently, polite, earnest, and enormously well intentioned. There were calls for "world-class standards." A private organization, largely controlled and funded by major businesses, was organized to promote, coordinate, and, to the greatest possible extent, calibrate children's scores on standardized tests across the nation, thus enabling a national, state-by-state "report card." The existence of this "report card" would stir up the competitive juices of states to do whatever was necessary to get their kids' scores up. "World-class standards" were, apparently, assumed to be the same thing as high scores on standardized tests. The conferees called for the people to follow them in this quest for better schools. Most major state and city governments did. Many locals were not so sure.

Needless to say, Deborah Meier is not so sure. Her paper raises many of the profound philosophical and practical issues that present challenges to much current central government policy. Let me extend some of Meier's argument in two directions.

WHO HAS THE RIGHT
TO CONTROL MY CHILD'S MIND?

The community does, to some degree: I cannot educate my child to be insensitive to the collective needs, socially accepted restraints and agreements of the people with whom she lives. The character of knowledge ("science," broadly defined) necessarily affects my child: she is likely to make good sense of the world by standing on the shoulders of smart people who have earlier struggled to give rational shape to our surroundings. As a parent, I have a duty to see that my child reflects both my values and those reasonably reflective of what I believe to be the best within the larger community. My child's mind is my responsibility, at least until that earlier-than-I-might-like day when my child begins to make up her own mind.

Virtually all American parents want their children "schooled," that is, to be given the tools and attitudes necessary to flourish into adulthood. Beyond the obvious matters of literacy, numeracy, and fundamental understandings of civics, thoughtful and decent people can disagree, especially about the secondary school curriculum. For example, some will insist that each of their children master calculus. Others will not, arguing that calculus is important for only a small minority of adults. Some will want their children immersed early in controversial texts, ones that (these parents believe) may help ready them for shocks that reality will deal them in but a few years. Other parents may want to protect their children as long as possible from any sort of shock. Still others will seek some middle ground. Some parents will want their children exposed to the ideas of Charles Darwin and to the evidence of the validity of his ideas. Others will not. The list is almost endless. Because these matters are only partly of science and as much of the heart, single answers to such questions are never universally acceptable. As a result, every parent—whatever his or her income and educational level—wants a substantial say about these issues. The ideas to which our children are exposed are important. Our right to control many, if not all, of these ideas deserves to be a fundamental American freedom.

Arrogation of this right by central governments is an abridgment of freedom. The myriad, detailed, and mandated state "curriculum frameworks," of whatever scholarly brilliance, are attacks on intellectual freedom. "High-stakes" tests arising from these curricula compound the felony. Yes, the community has the right to impose some common values, ones that make our freedom a practical reality. And, yes, the community must expect civility and a readiness to compromise when compromise is essential. That said, it is the apparent readiness of contemporary government to reach beyond this that signals government's failure to respect and trust its own people. Without such trust, there can be no democracy.

As Deborah Meier tells us, freedom is messy. The disagreements over important ideas cause tensions; but such tensions, and the willingness to confront and work through them, lie at the heart of democracy. Meier goes even further: the students' observation of how adults come to collective understanding in the face of those disagreements is itself a powerful and worthy lesson.

Simply, the detailed contours of culture—and, willy-nilly, schools are crucibles of culture—are too important to be given to central authorities unilaterally to define and then to impose. Yes, there must be compromises between what I want and what the community wants. However, I personally want to be a party to the definition of those compromises. Yes, there is the matter of empirical evidence: I cannot simply walk away from such evidence when it suits my prejudices. However, I expect that government will never assume that it always knows best.

I know that we all cannot agree all the time. Save at the obvious margins, why should we? Variety is no sin. For my child I would like a choice among schools that play out the necessary compromises between the values of the state and those to which I am thoughtfully committed. From among these I can elect a school that reflects my deepest and fairest sense of the culture in which I wish my child to grow up.

This sort of parental authority and choice is well established for wealthy American families. By choosing to live in a culturally congenial district or selecting a private school, they can buy whatever education seems best to them. If such choices make sense for rich folks—and rich folks will fight hard to protect their right to choose their children's schools—why not make them available to everybody? Intellectual freedom doesn't stop at the door of a bank. Intellectual freedom is what characterizes a confident, mature democracy. Intellectual freedom reflects the trust of government in the ultimate wisdom of its people.

What Is a School?

For many of us it is a building into which children go for a portion of their time, say, 190 days a year or "990 hours a year of delivered instruction" (as one state bluntly defines it). A school is a place where children are gathered under the force of the law to pursue the learning of what the community believes is important.

Of course, children, and especially older children and adolescents, learn much more outside of school than within it. Kids watch us all the time, learning from what they see, admiring (or not) what we do and how we do it, whether we are family members or neighbors or representations of people and places displayed in the media. That is why "child care" is such an enormously important profession.

If what is "outside" of school rewards a child and gives access to that which is valued within school, a symbiosis results. If the "outside" neglects what the place called school values, the child is at best confused in school—"How could this be important when I see so few people in my own neighborhood valuing it?"—and at worst a failure in the school's eyes. For whatever they are worth, test scores and truancy rates tell this story.

For fifty years, government has evolved policies that assume basically common approaches for teaching youngsters from kindergarten through twelfth grade. As a result, patterns of practice, such as daily attendance, and rituals, such as enthusiastic "support" of one's school as a premier, valued, and special place, are commonly applied to young people from age five to age eighteen. Differences are represented (little kids may be bused to school, older kids expected to make do on public transportation) but the commonalities persist. When most people talk of "public education," they make few serious distinctions between what is due the very young and what is due their teenaged elders. The result, not surprisingly, is Procrustean.

Deborah Meier is unusual in that she has designed and led both elementary and secondary public schools. Each is a "place," and each fiercely protects its own boundaries. All are schools of choice. All are small, self-conscious communities. All expect to be alliances of teachers, children, parents, and their relevant neighborhoods. All are places where the necessarily endless confrontation of important ideas about which people may disagree proceeds in a respectful way; they are places where relationships are as important as abstractions are. All have sophisticated notions of what intellectual excellence is and therefore how it might be represented. All aim ultimately at "enduring and worthy habits of mind," at what sort of thinking adults these young people may become, at how they think and act when no one is looking. To the limit of their school systems' regulation, all connect their students with the world beyond them. All are intensely demanding, of everyone involved.

Nonetheless, even such imaginative places touch predominantly the "school-going time" of their students. Secondary school students may hold internships and more, but the metaphor is a young person leaving "the place" to get something to bring back. The needed next step is to perceive of the formal education of adolescents, especially of older adolescents, as comprising on an equal basis both a "place" and "outside" opportunities beyond it.

Perhaps, with all good intentions, we Americans infantilize our older teenagers by holding them to the same sorts of routines and standards as those for the younger. The policy hammerlock on the definitions of the substance of a high school education deplored by Meier needs to be broken. But perhaps also we need a fundamental redefinition of the obligations a growing adolescent must accept for himself and for the community of which he is a part, and then of what structures will help him reach of those obligations. Most adolescents are eager to take responsibility. They deserve our imaginative effort to give them the opportunity to express it in constructive ways, ones that help them build principled and informed minds.

Simply, it may be not enough only to refine what is best for high schools. It may be better to redefine what is best for the learning of our older children.

Such a prospect is miles away from the school world implied by the proceedings at the recent education "summit." The assumptions there were familiar and predictable and represented devices used with limited success for fifty years. Something bolder, more democratic, and more reflective of the realities of growing up in a modern, information-rich society is badly needed. Deborah Meier has started us down that important road.

3

REPLY

DEBORAH MEIER

I recently came across a speech by Joseph Priestley given on the dedication of New College, in London, in 1794:

Whatever be the qualifications of your tutors, your improvement must chiefly depend on yourselves. They cannot think or labour for you, they can only put you in the best way of thinking and labouring for yourselves. If therefore you get knowledge you must acquire it by your own industry. You must form all conclusions and all maxims for yourselves, from premises and data collected and considered by yourself. And it is the great object of this institution to remove every bias the mind may be under, and to give the greatest scope for true freedom of thinking and equity.

If becoming an educated person depends, as Priestley says, upon one's own industry, how best can we engage the industry of youngsters, and their communities, in their own behalf? This question lies at the heart of democratic society—even more than in Priestley's time. Priestley could dismiss the laggards as unfit for a good education. We cannot.

But what should we do? Should we rely on efficiency, prescription, and compliance as a means for meeting Priestley's challenge? That is the central issue in this debate, and the thread that runs through the principal challenges advanced in the responses to my essay.

1. Don't I know that standards are meant to ensure equity for the least advantaged? I never doubted that this was one important motive. (It was assumption number five in my essay.) Yes, standardization and centralized control have often been hallmarks of efforts on behalf of the oppressed.

But when it comes to schooling, this approach is not sound. I believe that we have hard evidence that the best reform strategy involves reinventing schools on the model of the small, locally grounded schools I know best. The last thing we need is more of the centralization and standardization that has always dominated schools (and classrooms) serving the poor. That has been part of the problem.

Abigail Thernstrom is right that in this respect I sound like a defender of private school privilege. Except that I want to extend some of that privilege (including more autonomy) to the urban schools that so many low-income minority students attend, and that traditionally possess the least autonomy from centralized authority.

The shift away from local control even in our more prosperous communities, and the demise of experiments with meaningful on-site power in poor communities, is dramatic. With what results? Unlike Richard Murnane I see no convincing evidence that centralization in North Carolina and Texas has produced significant gains. While scores on the Texas Assessment of Academic Skills (TASS) test have gone up on account of the state's relentless pursuit of test-driven curriculum and teaching, Texas students are scoring the same, or lower, on nationally normed tests. And the impact of these reforms on graduation rates for precisely the students Murnane is most concerned with remain unknown—but potentially scary.

Contrary to what Gary Nash says, lots of people are looking to make standards de facto national and mandatory—from textbook publishers (who are also our test publishers), who have long homogenized our educational fare, to a new host of reformers who see in even the occasional oddball exceptions a danger to standards. They, unlike Murnane and Nash, are determined to cut off the escape valves.

2. What about the dangers of local control? Nash and Thernstrom warn that local control often means right-wing and bigoted (for example, the recent decision in Kansas to stop teaching evolution). True enough, local empowerment can often be vicious and retrograde. But so too can nationally imposed power. We apparently disagree in our assessment of the danger to democratic life or schooling of tipping the scales still further in the direction of centralization.

Again, this is a disagreement over a fundamental assumption. I think the benefits of greater autonomy and more local control outweigh its dangers when it comes to schools. My long-term fundamental faith in local democracy, and a recognition that there are sufficient incentives in place—such as the requirements of employers and universities, as Murnane points out—that keep local school standards from straying too far afield makes me rest easier than my critics. I'm more nervous that few will stray far enough!

I apologize to Nash if my remarks in favor of local control sound like "disdain for the efforts of university-based scholars to involve themselves in K-12 education." We do need them. And we need them also in the reform of college education, which too often fails our neediest students in the same way that many of our big comprehensive high schools do.

3. But don't we need some standards? Central Park East was perhaps the first public school in the nation to graduate students only on the basis of standards—not classroom hours logged, but publicly evaluated performances. We are not debating the value of standards, but *how* to raise them and who should decide them.

I agree with all of Bob Chase's highly reasonable conditions for standards-based reform. I believe all will require a less grandiose state role. The state, and the academy, should nudge, persuade, expose, even embarrass, but do so from a far deeper analysis than we get from test scores. The state, like the academy, can lead the way in promoting higher standards—offering richer and deeper resources, especially for staff development. Teachers need far more well-crafted time to examine their work—as Nash, Chase, and Murnane all point out.

I welcome standards that "provide guidelines, and perhaps some inspiration, for those interested" (Nash). I read the California early standards efforts with much interest and borrowed, when I was at the Central Park East, many features of them. We do need experts out there, talking about what is worth knowing. But Chester Finn is partly right: if the teachers in our schools, and ultimately their communities, don't see our standards as theirs, then we "aren't going anywhere." And shouldn't. If parents think "character" and "extracurricular life" are as important as "academics," maybe schools should listen. I hope Nash will join me in fighting off efforts to turn some cobbled-together compromise between interesting, useful, competing viewpoints into the one "correct" view of what it means to be well educated.

4. But if you agree that we need higher standards, why not use standardized tests? Thernstrom's rhetoric and tone reflect the harshness many of the central authorities feel they must take on behalf of their draconian testing policies. I don't think she actually believes that my opposition to tests means that I am as unconcerned about the have-nots as her words suggest, or that I favor low standards for low-income kids.

But she does believe that the tests—even some of the sillier ones Massachusetts has adopted—fairly measure the only important qualities of a well-educated person, and that they must be imposed at all costs. That my New York students' subsequent life histories are not indicated by their SAT scores, which were never much affected by the school's work—despite Kaplan-sponsored test coaching—doesn't puzzle her. She's stuck on measuring merit by one, and only one, criterion even when the evidence tells her otherwise. As though the purpose of schools were test scores based on schooling, not life scores based on living.

She further suggests that maybe I'm not a trustworthy

spokesperson for low-income students since students at Mission Hill had reading scores on the Iowa Basic Skills third-grade reading test that placed them below the state median. In fact, our students scored at the sixty-second percentile on this nationally normed measure—not bad for an "inner-city" school. But we pay more attention to our own harder data—taped-recorded, one-on-one reading exams we give in the fall and spring to all our students. By this measure virtually all our students are fluent readers by the end of fourth grade. In crying wolf over Mission Hill's test scores, this member of the Massachusetts Board of Education endangers a success that ought to be getting some attention. But her error is revealing: defenders of high-stakes testing keep telling us that education is in crisis, and keep neglecting all the evidence that refutes their extreme assertions of doom.

The success of Mission Hill is a happy reminder of a time and place in our educational history when we were promoting professional judgment. It benefits as well from an apparently short-lived interest in beating off charters by offering an in-district form of chartering called "pilot schools." But how long can Mission Hill and other Boston pilots survive if their initiatives are undermined by ever-more-detailed state mandates—about subjects to be taught, material to be covered, time to be spent per subject (down to the minute)—and a single high-stakes test as a measure of success? And what if indicators that are far more significantly correlated to later college and life success for low-income and African-American youngsters are no longer counted, and reforms guided by them die out? For example, while going to a small school correlates with later success in school, it does not substantially raise test scores. Other indicators turn out to be more attainable and equally powerful: perseverance, high attendance, strong relationships with adults outside the family, and participation in extracurricular and service-learning experiences. Smallness also correlates with school safety and a greater sense of personal efficacy. How sad if we lose track of these in our relentless pursuit of test scores.

I welcomed Bill Ayers's comments on behalf of our shared vision and his analysis of the impact of standardization on Chicago's neediest. Like Ayers, I know that our schools all need a jolt, and I suspect we both welcome such shocks even when they come in the wrong ways. I've watched Linda Nathan's work—and that of her colleague Larry Myatt—for years. Nathan's Fenway school started up at the same time as Central Park East, and we gave each other encouragement and inspiration. She's probably right that what I'm proposing shouldn't be an alternative, but what we ought to see as the mainstream.

So too is the charter school that Ted and Nancy Sizer helped found in Fort Devens, Massachusetts. Ted Sizer, above all people, helped me to see the value of not agreeing on a single definition of a good school. In fact, close as our views so often are, we didn't design the same secondary school when we had the chance. And our graduating standards are not duplicates of each other's. We probably chose not to send our kids to the same schools, and we did not ourselves attend schools with the same "standards"—"save at the obvious margins." Figuring out those "obvious margins" is a heady task, and one we ought to be engaged in, instead of developing ever-longer laundry lists of what every eight-, ten-, fourteen-, and eighteen-year-old should know and be tested on—or off with her head.

I agree with Sizer that "990 hours a year of delivered instruction" is just a drop in the bucket. What has always amazed me is how powerful that drop can be—if we use our hearts and minds. But, as Priestley would have noted, you can't force hearts and minds. They must labor on their own behalves. My concern about standardization and high-stakes testing stems precisely from my conviction that what makes some schools overcome the limitations of time is the power of the relationships that are developed inside them: among members of the faculty, between young people and adults, and finally among young people. Only a very powerful faculty can build those enduring and rigorous relationships with the young; only a faculty that also accepts responsibility for developing its own standards will be tough enough to police its own kids and its own colleagues. Schools that do less cannot offer enough to overcome the odds facing too many youngsters.

ABOUT THE CONTRIBUTORS

WILLIAM AYERS is Distinguished Professor of Education at the University of Illinois at Chicago. His latest book is *A Kind and Just Parent: The Children of Juvenile Court*.

BOB CHASE is president of the National Education Association, which represents 2.4 million public school teachers and support staff across the country.

JONATHAN KOZOL taught for three years in the public schools of Boston and Newton, Massachusetts; for seven years he worked in alternative schools that grew out of the civil rights struggles of the 1960s and the early 1970s. He is the author of the National Book Award winner *Death at an Early Age* and the Anisfield-Wolf Book Award winner *Amazing Grace: The Lives of Children and the Conscience of a Nation*. His forthcoming book on children and their spiritual beliefs is *Ordinary Resurrections*.

DEBORAH MEIER is the principal of a pilot Boston public school. She began her career as a kindergarten teacher in Chicago. She was the founder of the Central Park East elementary and secondary schools, vice-chair of the Coalition of Essential Schools, and is author of *The Power of Their Ideas*. In 1987 she received the prestigious MacArthur grant for her work in East Harlem.

RICHARD J. MURNANE, an economist, is the Thompson Professor of Education and Society at the Harvard Graduate School of Education. His most recent book, written with MIT professor Frank Levy, is entitled *Teaching the New Basic Skills*.

GARY B. NASH is professor of history at UCLA, former president of the Organization of American Historians, and director of the National Center for History in the Schools.

LINDA NATHAN is the current and first headmaster of Boston Arts Academy, a pilot high school in the Boston Public Schools. She was the cofounder of the Center for Collaborative Education–Metro Boston.

ABOUT THE CONTRIBUTORS

THEODORE SIZER is founder and charman of the Coalition of Essential Schools and acting principal, with his wife, Nancy, of the Francis W. Parker School in Fort Devens, Massachusetts. He is coauthor of *The Students Are Watching: Schools and the Moral Contract.*

ABIGAIL THERNSTROM is a member of the Massachusetts Board of Education and coauthor of *America in Black and White: One Nation, Indivisible.*